T0197144

Wounded Soul: A Church Abuse Journal

AUTUMN D. WILLIAMS M.A.

authorHOUSE®

AuthorHouse™
1663 Liberty Drive
Bloomington, IN 47403
www.authorhouse.com
Phone: 833-262-8899

© 2023 Autumn D. Williams M.A. All rights reserved.

No part of this book may be reproduced, stored in a retrieval system, or transmitted by any means without the written permission of the author.

Published by AuthorHouse 12/13/2022

ISBN: 978-1-6655-7713-7 (sc)
ISBN: 978-1-6655-7711-3 (hc)
ISBN: 978-1-6655-7712-0 (e)

Print information available on the last page.

Any people depicted in stock imagery provided by Getty Images are models, and such images are being used for illustrative purposes only.
Certain stock imagery © Getty Images.

This book is printed on acid-free paper.

Because of the dynamic nature of the Internet, any web addresses or links contained in this book may have changed since publication and may no longer be valid. The views expressed in this work are solely those of the author and do not necessarily reflect the views of the publisher, and the publisher hereby disclaims any responsibility for them.

Dedication

This work is dedicated to my family and friends. It is also dedicated to those who shared in the life experiences that caused the understanding of church abuse to be possible. Thank you!

Introduction

Let's make healing form church hurt a movement. When I say healing, I mean it respectfully. I am not saying that it has to look a certain way. Oftentimes people do not understand how to deal with pain or those who have trouble processing it. It is often like God, you can't see it, however, you can trace the effects of it. In some cases, it is not safe to tell the full extent of your story until you are strong enough to do so. It is good to be mindful who to share it with and if at all possible, with a trusted licensed professional. This is just one humble tool to help you on your journey. This is written in question-and-answer form, so you can take some time to ponder on your experiences

Lastly, I believe that if you choose this book, you have not given up. I want you to know that I am so proud of you! Do not let anything stand in your way of experiencing freedom from church hurt!

Sometimes getting things out helps the healing process. What is your story with church abuse?

What was the first or most significant abuse that you felt from church?

Do you feel that what you experienced with church abuse was something malicious or done intentionally? Provide details.

Was there anything that you could have done differently, so that you did not experience this?

If there was something that you could have done differently, do you blame yourself?

Has experiencing church hurt stopped your momentum or zeal for life? If so, how?

What are three things that you can do to regain your momentum?

What things did you learn from the abuse you encountered?

Do you feel the abuse weakened you? Why or why not?

What strengths did you gain from it?

Are there ways that you could think of what you experienced differently? Provide details.

What steps can you take not to feel victimized if you have ever felt that way?

Is there anything that you want to repent for, in reaction to the abuse that you received at church?

What specific things do you feel you should do, but can't because of the trauma of church hurt?

Are there situations occurring that seem similar to what you experienced?

Are they actually similar or does something about the situation seem similar?

Do you feel that something about you attracted the abuse, whether in your personality, past or family line?

Have you forgiven the individuals who abused you? Why or why not? If you have, what was this experience like? If you have not, is that your desire? If it is a desire, what do you think this process would look like?

Did the incident cause you to be angry with God?

What are your thoughts about this?

Have you tried to protect yourself? Has it been beneficial to you?

Is it possible that the person who hurt you had good intentions? If this is a possibility, how does it make you feel?

Do you feel what happened occurred while you were in a state of vulnerability? If so, what can you take from this experience?

Initially In your heart, did you feel a desire to not be around the person who abused you? What has it taught you about your intuition?

How does your pain affect you? How does your pain affect others?

What are some things that you can do to look at what you experienced in a positive light?

What hurts you the most about your experience?

Do you have known fears directly associated with what occurred? Do you feel it is possible to overcome these fears? If so, how? If not, why not?

Do you ever feel physical pain or discomfort because of what happened? If so, explain this experience. What are you doing to address this?

Are you apprehensive about going to church again?

After your experience, were you rejected or ostracized? How do you feel about the event? Did you feel unprotected in what you experienced?

Was there something in your upbringing that caused you to be attracted to the church environment where you experienced abuse? If so, what was it? Has it changed?

Were you underage when the abuse happened? If so, how did it affect your growth?

If people learned that you were abused, what was it like for you? Did you learn anything?

Did the incident cause you to feel differently about God? Explain.

Did you feel like God had abused you when you experienced pain from church? Explain.

Did you feel manipulated to give? If so, how did this affect your life? How did it affect you emotionally?

Do you feel like you experienced shame? Why or why not?

Some people experience multiple painful things in church. What was the worst thing you experienced?

How did the experience change your life?

Are you expecting an apology? What will the outcome be if you do not get one?

Did what you experience cause self-hatred? If it did, explain.

If it didn't, what did it cause you to feel?

Do you hate or blame God for what you experienced? Why or why not?

Who is your support system? Have they aided you with the abuse that occurred? If so, how?

What is your strategy for recovery? If you do not have a strategy, what are some things that you can implement to heal?

Do you feel like you went through a grieving process for any loss you experienced while coming out of the spiritually abusive environment? Expound on this.

Do you feel like your fellow believers have understood your process? What was their reaction to your experiences? Did you hope for them to react differently? Was your hope realistic?

Are there habits that you developed to cope? Would you consider them healthy? If they are not healthy, what other things can you do?

Do you feel like being in an abusive environment has changed you or your personality? How so? What does it look like to alter this difference? What were you like before experiencing church hurt?

Have you been able to go to church since the abuse? If not, do you want to go? What would make you comfortable there?

How would you rate your ability to trust? Explain. Would you like to see it improve? Why or why not? If you would like to see it improve, what steps do you feel are necessary to make it a reality?

Has your self-esteem been affected by the abuse you experienced? If so, what will you do to regain confidence?

Printed in the United States
by Baker & Taylor Publisher Services